JANICE VANCLEAVE'S
CRAZY, KOOKY, AND QUIRKY
BIOLOGY
EXPERIMENTS

Illustrations by
Jim Carroll

rosen publishing's
**rosen
central**

New York

This edition published in 2019 by
The Rosen Publishing Group, Inc.
29 East 21st Street
New York, NY 10010

Library of Congress Cataloging-in-Publication Data

Names: VanCleave, Janice Pratt, author.
Title: Janice VanCleave's crazy, kooky, and quirky biology experiments / Janice VanCleave.
Description: New York : Rosen Central, 2019. | Series: Janice VanCleave's crazy, kooky, and quirky science experiments | Audience: Grades 5–8. | Includes bibliographical references and index.
Identifiers: LCCN 2017055528| ISBN 9781508180968 (library bound) | ISBN 9781508181019 (paperback)
Subjects: LCSH: Biology—Experiments—Juvenile literature.
Classification: LCC QH309.2 .V36 2019 | DDC 570.72/4—dc23
LC record available at https://lccn.loc.gov/2017055528

Manufactured in the United States of America

Experiments first published in *Janice VanCleave's 203 Icy, Freezing, Frosty, Cool, and Wild Experiments* by John Wiley & Sons, Inc. copyright © 1999 Janice VanCleave

CONTENTS

INTRODUCTION

Biology is the study of the way living organisms behave and interact. The people who decide to work in the field of biology have a variety of career choices. Some biologists work outdoors in remote ecosystems. Other scientists work in laboratories to study topics as varied as cures for diseases, new marine species, or human DNA. Zoologists study animals, and botanists study plants. Most biologists study life on Earth, but astrobiologists search for life outside our planet. All these people have something in common: they are constantly asking questions to learn even more about living things.

Earth has been supporting the tiniest of single-celled living things for as many as 3.5 billion years. Arthropods, fish, plants, and mammals came later. Humans evolved about two hundred thousand years ago. The mysterious, ever-changing nature of living organisms makes biology a fascinating branch of science.

This book is a collection of science experiments about biology. How does gravity affect blood flow in the body? Why are penguins' wings good for flying? How does temperature affect odor? You will find the answers to these and many other questions by doing the experiments in this book.

HOW TO USE THIS BOOK

You will be rewarded with successful experiments if you read each experiment carefully, follow the steps in order, and do not substitute materials. The following sections are included for all the experiments.

» **PURPOSE:** *The basic goals for the experiment.*

» **MATERIALS:** *A list of supplies you will need.* You will experience less frustration and more fun if you gather all the necessary materials for the experiments before you begin. You lose your train of thought when you have to stop and search for supplies.

» **PROCEDURE:** *Step-by-step instructions on how to perform the experiment.* Follow each step very carefully, never skip steps, and do not add your own. Safety is of the utmost importance, and by reading the experiment before starting, then following the instructions exactly, you can feel confident that no unexpected results will occur. Ask an adult to help you when you are working with anything sharp or hot. If adult supervision is required, it will be noted in the experiment.

» **RESULTS:** *An explanation stating exactly what is expected to happen.* This is an immediate learning tool. If the expected results are achieved, you will know that you did the experiment correctly. If your results are not the same as described in the experiment, carefully read the instructions and start over from the first step.

» **WHY?** *An explanation of why the results were achieved.*

INTRODUCTION

THE SCIENTIFIC METHOD

Scientists identify a problem or observe an event. Then they look for solutions or explanations through research and experimentation. By doing the experiments in this book, you will learn to follow experimental steps and make observations. You will also learn many scientific principles that have to do with biology.

In the process, the things you see or learn may lead you to new questions. For example, suppose you have completed the experiment that models an insect's compound eye. Now you wonder whether the distance from an object affects how well a compound eye works. That's great! All scientists are curious and ask new questions about what they learn. When you design a new experiment, it is a good idea to follow the scientific method.

1. Ask a question.

2. Do some research about your question. What do you already know?

3. Come up with a hypothesis, or a possible answer to your question.

4. Design an experiment to test your hypothesis. Make sure the experiment is repeatable.

5. Collect the data and make observations.

6. Analyze your results.

7. Reach a conclusion. Did your results support your hypothesis?

Many times the experiment leads to more questions and a new experiment. *Always remember that when devising your own science experiment, have a knowledgeable adult review it with you before trying it out. Ask him or her to supervise it as well.*

COATED

PURPOSE To demonstrate the effect that oil spills can have on birds.

MATERIALS 2 small bowls
tap water
3 tablespoons (45 ml) oil
two 2- to 3-inch (5- to 7.5 cm)-long feathers
(can be purchased at a crafts store)

NOTE: Do not pick up bird feathers from the ground outdoors. They can carry diseases.

PROCEDURE

1. Fill the bowls three-fourths full with water.

2. Pour the oil into one of the bowls.

3. Gently lay one of the feathers on the surface of the water in the bowl without the oil.

4. Lift the feather from the bowl and blow on it.

5. Gently lay the second feather on the surface of the oil in the second bowl.

6. Lift the feather from the bowl and blow on it.

RESULTS The feather taken from the water appears dry and is light enough to be moved by your breath. The feather taken from the oil appears wet and heavy. It moves little or not at all when you blow on it.

WHY? Water does not stick to the feathers of birds very easily, but oil does. The oil-coated feather is very heavy, and the fibers of the feather stick together. This experiment demonstrates how oil from oil spills can mat the feathers of birds and make the birds too heavy to fly. This makes the birds easy prey (animal hunted for food) to predators.

TOO MUCH, TOO FAST

PURPOSE To demonstrate the effect of overfishing.

MATERIALS

scissors
2 dishwashing sponges
ruler
large bowl of tap water
2 tea strainers—1 small, 1 large

small bowl
pencil
writing paper
helper

PROCEDURE

1. Cut each sponge into 1-inch (2.5 cm) cubes.

2. Place ten sponge cubes in the bowl of water, spreading the cubes over the water's surface.

3. Ask your helper to close his or her eyes and move the small strainer through the water once to scoop up as many cubes as possible.

4. Remove the cubes from the strainer and place them in the small bowl.

5. Count the cubes remaining in the water, and add an equal number of cubes to double the amount of cubes in the water.

6. Repeat steps 3 to 5 three times. On the last scooping, do not add any cubes. Record the number of cubes in the water.

7. Start over with ten cubes in the water.

8. Ask your helper to do steps 3 and 4 four times, using the large strainer. Do not add cubes between scoopings. After the last time,

count the cubes remaining in the water and add an equal number of cubes to double the amount of cubes in the water. Record the number of cubes.

RESULTS The number of cubes in the bowl of water increases when the small strainer is used and cubes are added after each scooping. The number of cubes greatly decreases and may even be zero after four scoops with the large strainer.

WHY? The sponge cubes represent fish and the strainers commercial fishing nets. Scooping with the small strainer is like fishing with fewer nets and catching fewer fish. Adding cubes represents reproduction of fish. Commercial fishing boats haul in more fish. Overfishing removes fish faster than they can reproduce, as demonstrated by using the large strainer and not adding cubes after each scooping. Some fish are in danger of becoming extinct (no longer in existence) because of overfishing.

SLOW SHUFFLE

PURPOSE To show how emperor penguins carry their eggs.

MATERIALS 1 cup (250 ml) dry rice
sock

PROCEDURE

1. Pour the rice into the sock.

2. Tie a knot in the sock.

3. Stand with your feet together.

4. Place the sock of rice on top of your feet.

5. Try to walk without dropping the sock off your feet.

RESULTS The sock stays on your feet only if you move short distances at a time.

WHY? Female emperor penguins lay one egg, which the male rolls on top of his feet. The egg stays in this position until it hatches, about two months later. To move around without dropping the egg, the penguin must do a slow shuffle like the shuffle you did with the sock of rice. But emperor penguins do have a little extra help from a flap of skin that folds down over the egg. This skin helps to keep the egg in place and also keeps it warm. Staying warm is difficult since emperor penguins hatch their eggs during the Antarctic winter, where winds at times blow in excess of 100 miles per hour (160 kph), and the temperature can drop to –80°F (–62°C). After the egg hatches, the male and female take turns carrying their baby chick around on their feet for about another two months. This keeps the chick from freezing until its fat layer and protective feathers develop.

PADDLES

PURPOSE To determine why penguins' wings are good for swimming.

MATERIALS scissors
ruler
sheet of printer paper
large bowl of water

PROCEDURE

1. Cut two 2-by-8-inch (5-by-20 cm) strips from the paper.

2. Holding one short end of one of the paper strips, try to push the water back and forth with the other end of the strip.

3. Fold the second paper strip in half from side to side. Fold it again from top to bottom.

4. Repeat step 2, using the folded paper.

RESULTS The folded paper pushes the water back and forth, while the unfolded paper bends and doesn't push the water very well.

WHY? The unfolded paper bends as it moves through the water, much like the wings of most birds. Thus, these wings are not useful for swimming. The folded paper easily pushes the water back and forth. Like the paper, the wings of a penguin are small and stiff, and act like paddles as they push the penguin through the water.

DIVERS

PURPOSE To determine how the density of a penguin's body affects its diving and swimming ability.

MATERIALS

1-quart (1 liter) widemouthed jar
tap water
1-tablespoon (15 ml) measuring spoon
3 tablespoons (45 ml) table salt

2 empty film canisters or small
    plastic vials with caps
masking tape
pen
ruler

PROCEDURE

1. Fill the jar with water.

2. Pour 1 tablespoon (15 ml) of salt in one of the canisters and close the lid.

3. Use the masking tape and pen to label the canister 1.

4. Add 2 tablespoons (30 ml) of salt to the other film canister, close its lid, and label it 2.

5. Place the canisters in the jar of water. Observe the level where each floats in the water.

6. Remove the canisters from the water, hold canister 1 about 2 inches (5 cm) above the water, then drop it.

7. Observe how far the canister sinks in the water.

8. Repeat steps 6 and 7, using canister 2.

RESULTS When canister 1 is floating, it leans, and less of it is below the water than canister 2. When dropped into the water, canister 2 sinks to a deeper depth and takes longer to rise than does canister 1.

WHY? The canisters are the same size, but canister 2 is heavier because the extra salt gives it more mass (the amount of material in an object). Thus, canister 2 has a greater density, or mass per volume, than canister 1.The greater the density of an object, the more easily it sinks in water. Penguins are heavier than most birds. This body weight is partly due to their solid, heavy bones. Unlike penguins, which don't fly, flying birds have light bones filled with lots of air. The penguins' heavier weight makes it easier for them to dive deeper. They also float lower in the water, which lets them use their powerful wings to push themselves along. Lighter birds that float high in the water can only use their feet to push themselves along when they swim.

COILED

PURPOSE To model the movement of the feeding tube of butterflies and moths.

MATERIALS party blower

PROCEDURE

1. Place the party blower upside down in your mouth so that the end hangs down and coils toward your body.

2. Blow into the tube, then suck the air out.

RESULTS The party blower uncoils, then coils again.

WHY? The proboscis (feeding tube) of butterflies and moths stays coiled under the insect's head when not in use. To uncoil the tube, blood from the insect's body is forced into the proboscis, similar to the way you forced air into the party blower. When uncoiled, the proboscis is used by the insect to reach into flowers and suck up nectar (a sugary liquid).

COILED FEEDING TUBE

Proboscis

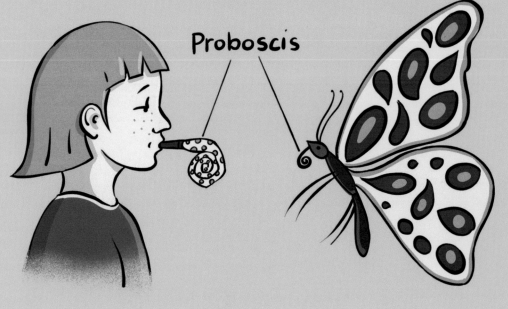

JUICY

PURPOSE To model how flies eat.

MATERIALS

eyedropper
baby food jar of sweet potatoes
craft stick

masking tape
pen

PROCEDURE

1. Place the tip of the eyedropper just below the surface of the potatoes in the jar. Try to fill the eyedropper with the sweet potatoes. Observe the amount of sweet potatoes that enter the eyedropper, if any.

2. Wash the eyedropper and allow it to dry.

3. Collect as much saliva in your mouth as possible, put the saliva on the craft stick, and transfer the saliva to the surface of the potatoes in the jar. Close the jar.

4. Using a pen and a piece of tape across the lid and down the sides of the jar, label the jar DO NOT EAT.

5. Place the jar in the refrigerator and leave it undisturbed for one day.

6. After twenty-four hours, remove the jar from the refrigerator and repeat step 1.

RESULTS On your first try, you can draw little or no potatoes into the eyedropper. After the saliva has been in the jar for twenty-four hours, the potatoes at the surface are liquid. You can then easily draw them into the eyedropper.

WHY? Human saliva (liquid that softens and breaks down food), like the saliva of flies and many other insects, contains a chemical called amylase. Amylase breaks down starch, a complex chemical found in many foods, into less complex chemicals. In the experiment, the amylase in your saliva digested (broke down into an absorbable form) the potatoes, turning them to liquid. As you did in the experiment, flies drop saliva on the food they plan to eat. The amylase in the fly saliva quickly begins to digest the starch in the food. The spongy end of the fly's proboscis then soaks up the liquid and the insect sucks it in through the tube.

SINGERS

PURPOSE To model how crickets make sounds.

MATERIALS index card

fingernail file or emery board

PROCEDURE

1. Hold the index card upright so that one long edge rests on a table.

2. Support the card with one hand as you quickly draw the rough side of the file across the top edge of the card two times.

3. Wait one second and repeat steps 1 and 2.

RESULTS You hear a rasping sound.

WHY? When you rub the file across the paper, the rough surface of the file plucks the paper's edge, causing it to vibrate. The vibrating paper produces sound. Certain insects, like crickets and grasshoppers, produce sounds in much the same way. These insects make sounds by rubbing two body parts, usually one sharp-edged and the other rough or file-like, against each other. This process is called stridulation.

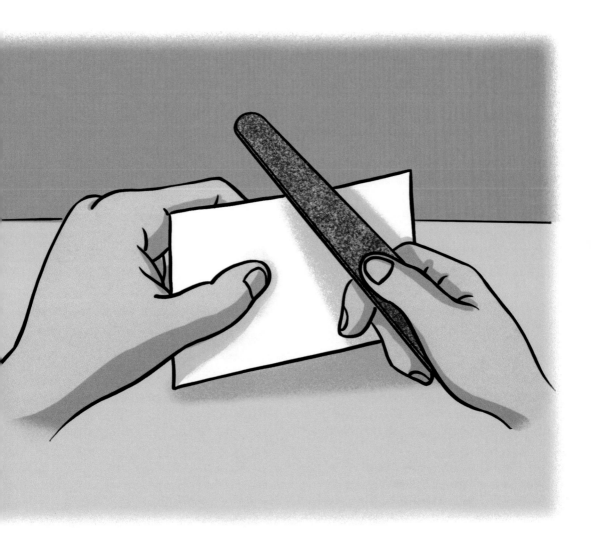

CLINGERS

PURPOSE To model how fleas hold on to their hosts.

MATERIALS scissors
ruler
10 feet (3 m) of heavy yarn or rug yarn
masking tape
4-by-8-inch (10-by-20 cm) piece of cardboard
medium-tooth comb

PROCEDURE

1. Cut a 6-inch (15 cm) piece from one end of the yarn and set it aside.

2. Spread the fingers of one hand apart and wrap the remaining yarn around your fingers.

3. Remove the loop of yarn from your hand.

4. Tie the strands together with the small, 6-inch (15 cm) piece of yarn.

5. Tape the ends of the small piece of yarn to the center of one short end of the cardboard.

6. Cut the bottom of the loop so that you have straight pieces of yarn.

7. Lay the cardboard on a table.

8. Holding the taped end of the yarn, push the teeth of the comb into the yarn. Try to comb the yarn.

RESULTS The comb sticks in the yarn.

WHY? The teeth of the comb are not spaced apart widely enough to easily pass through the yarn. A flea has spiny structures on its head similar to the teeth of the comb. The flea's spiny head sticks in the thick hair or fur of animals, the way the comb stuck in the yarn, keeping the flea from falling off the animal.

3-D

PURPOSE To make a model of an adult insect's three main body parts.

MATERIALS

4-ounce (113 g) stick of clay
sheet of paper
ruler
table knife

round toothpick
pencil
4-by-8-inch (10-by-20 cm) unruled
   index card

PROCEDURE

1. Lay the clay on the paper. Roll the clay into a tube 6 inches (15 cm) long.

2. Use the knife to cut the clay roll into three pieces: 1 inch (2.5 cm), 2 inches (5 cm), and 3 inches (7.5 cm) long.

3. Round the ends of each piece of clay.

4. Break the toothpick in half. Use one half of the toothpick to connect the 1-inch (2.5 cm) piece of clay to the 2-inch (5 cm) piece. Push the two clay pieces together so they touch.

5. Use the remaining half of the toothpick to connect the 3-inch (7.5 cm) piece of clay to the free end of the 2-inch (5 cm) piece. Push the clay pieces together as before.

6. Lay the connected clay pieces on the paper and mold them into the shape of an insect's body as shown.

7. Place the clay model on the index card and label the parts as shown.

RESULTS You have made a three-dimensional model of an insect's main body parts.

WHY? An adult insect's body is divided into three main body parts: the head, the thorax, and the abdomen. The head is the front part, the thorax is the middle part, and the abdomen is the hind part. Every insect has the same three body parts.

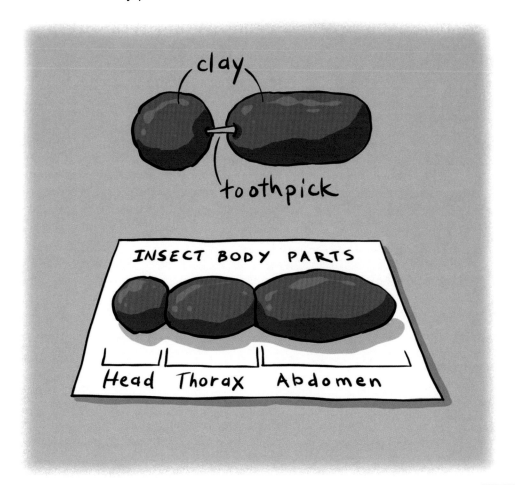

BOY OR GIRL?

PURPOSE To identify the gender (sex) of a cricket.

MATERIALS sharpened pencil
1-quart (1 liter) resealable plastic bag
8 to 10 crickets (can be purchased at a pet store)
magnifying lens

PROCEDURE

1. Prepare a temporary observing bag by using the point of the pencil to make 15 to 20 small air holes through both layers of the top of the bag.

2. Place one cricket in the bag.

3. Hold the cricket still by gently pressing the bag against its body. Use the magnifying lens to study the hind end of the cricket. Use the figures shown to determine if the cricket is a male or a female.

4. Within five minutes, remove the cricket from the observing bag.

5. Repeat steps 2 through 4 to identify the sex of each of the remaining crickets.

RESULTS Some of the crickets are identified as male and some as female.

WHY? You can tell male crickets from female crickets by looking at their abdomens. Every cricket has two feelers on its hind end, but the female has a third tube. It looks sort of like a stinger, but it's not. It's an egg-laying tube called an ovipositor.

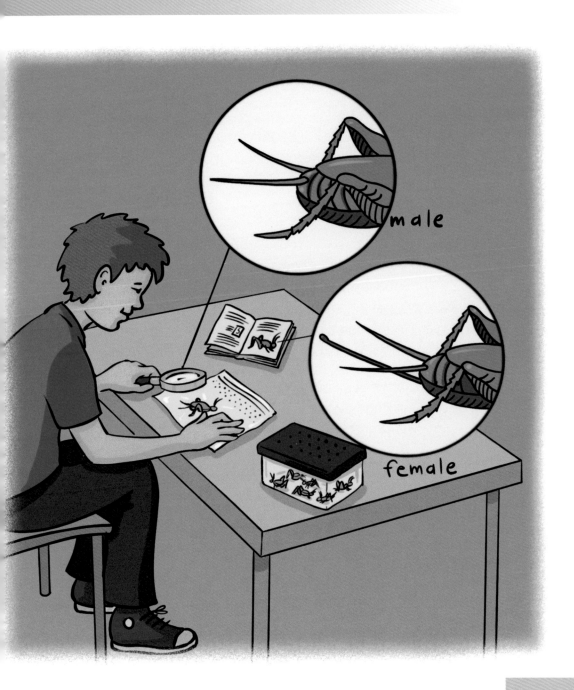

male

female

Boy or Girl?

LIFTERS

PURPOSE To demonstrate how handling a butterfly affects its ability to fly.

MATERIALS ruler

1-by-8-inch (2.5-by-20 cm) strip of printer paper
six ¾-inch (1.9 cm) round color-coding labels, three different colors
scissors

PROCEDURE

1. About 2 inches (5 cm) from one short end of the paper strip, place a row of two labels of the same color side by side. The first label should go next to the long edge of the paper strip. The second label will stick out from the opposite edge.

2. Add two more rows of different colored labels across the paper. Start each row on the opposite edge of the paper, and overlap the labels in the previous row, as shown.

3. Cut off the parts of the labels that stick out from the edges of the paper. This strip will be your butterfly wing.

4. Hold the end near the labels against your chin, just below your bottom lip. Blow hard just above the top of the paper and observe the movement of the paper.

5. Bend up one or two of the labels near your mouth, then repeat step 4.

RESULTS When you blow on the paper with the labels flat, the paper lifts, but the paper does not lift when the labels are bent up.

WHY? The paper lifts when you blow over it because of the change in air pressure. (Pressure is the amount of force on an area.) The faster-moving air above the paper produces lower pressure than the slower-moving air below the paper. The paper moves from the area of high pressure to the area of low pressure. This upward force on the paper due to the flow of air over it is called lift. Insects that fly use lift. Butterflies and other flying insects, such as moths, have tiny colored scales on their wings. Touching a butterfly can remove or bend the scales. This can make it hard for the insect to fly, the same way that bending the labels makes it hard for the paper to lift.

WATER WALKERS

PURPOSE To model water-walking insects.

MATERIALS scissors
1-by-3-inch (2.5-by-7.5 cm) strip of corrugated
cardboard (from a box)
pen
ruler
12-inch (30 cm) cotton terry stem (special pipe
cleaners available at craft stores), or use a
chenille craft stem (available at craft stores)
petroleum jelly (if using chenille craft stem)
large bowl of tap water

PROCEDURE

1. Cut the cardboard strip into an insect shape as shown. Draw eyes on one end of the strip.

2. Cut three 4-inch (10 cm) pieces from the cotton terry stem. If using a chenille craft stem, coat the sections with petroleum jelly.

3. Stick the pieces of stem all the way through three cardboard grooves in the middle section of the insect's body so that the same amount of stem sticks out on either side.

4. Bend each leg down where it meets the insect's body. Then, bend out about ¼ inch (0.63 cm) of the end of each leg to form a foot. Stand the insect on a table and adjust the bends in the legs so that each foot touches the table.

5. Slowly lower the insect into the water until its feet touch the surface of the water, then release it.

RESULTS The insect stands on the water's surface.

WHY? The molecules of water cling together at the surface to form a skin-like film. The attractive force that causes this is called surface tension. Because water has surface tension, some lightweight bugs can walk across the surface without sinking. At first, the terry stems in this experiment, like the hair covering the bodies of some water bugs, do not get wet. Unlike the hairs on a water insect, the terry stems in time do become wet and the model insect sinks.

BUG-EYED

PURPOSE To model an insect's eye.

MATERIALS scissors
cardboard tube from toilet tissue
24 drinking straws
transparent tape

PROCEDURE

1. Cut a slit down the tube so that it opens.

2. Stand the straws together on a flat surface and wrap the tube around the straws. Secure the tube with tape.

3. Hold the free end of the tube near, but not touching, your eye.

4. Close one eye and look through the tube with your open eye. Look at a moving object, such as the rotating blades of a fan.

5. As you continue to look through the tube, slowly move it to arm's length away from your body.

RESULTS Tiny separate images are seen through the straws.

WHY? Most insects have two large eyes called compound eyes, one on each side of the head. These eyes are made up of thousands of separate units called ommatidia. At the surface of each ommatidium is a lens called a facet. (A lens is a part of the eye that focuses light rays.) The ommatidia are grouped together so that the facets form a honeycomb pattern. Each ommatidium receives a small amount of light from the total

34

scene that the insect sees. These separate images are sent to the brain, where they are combined to form the whole picture. Scientists don't know what an insect actually sees. This experiment gives you an idea of what it might be like to receive images from the multiple facets of a compound eye.

Bug-Eyed

FLY AWAY

PURPOSE To model how some young spiders move to a new area.

MATERIALS scissors
ruler
spool of sewing thread
six ¾-inch (1.9 cm) round color-coding labels

PROCEDURE

1. Cut six pieces of thread, each about 6 inches (15 cm) long.

2. Attach one end of a thread to one of the labels by folding the label, sticky sides together, over the end of the thread. You have made a model of a spiderling.

3. Repeat step 2 five times to make five more spiderlings.

4. Lay the spiderlings together on a table.

5. Bend down toward the table so that your mouth is close to, but not touching, the spiderlings. Then, blow as hard as you can.

RESULTS The spiderlings fly away.

WHY? Some young spiders, or spiderlings, climb onto branches or other objects and release silk. As the silk lines lengthen, any wind lifts the small spider off its perch and it floats on the wind to a new area. This technique spiderlings use to float through the air and move to new areas is called ballooning. The flying models in this experiment represent ballooning spiderlings.

COVERED

PURPOSE To collect a spiderweb.

MATERIALS

black construction paper
small round plastic container, such as
   an empty, clean cottage cheese or
   margarine container

orb web (spiral shaped)
scissors
adult helper
spider field guide

PROCEDURE

1. Use the spider field guide to identify an orb web. These webs are often found between tree branches or porch pillars. Make sure the spider isn't in the web before doing the experiment.

2. Cut a circle from the construction paper to fit in the bottom of the plastic container and place it in the container.

3. Place the mouth of the container against the spiderweb.

4. Push the container forward to break off the part of the web covering the mouth of the container. Ask your helper to use the scissors to cut the web strands so that the web is stretched across the mouth of the container.

NOTE: Keep the web for the next experiment.

RESULTS A spiderweb is collected.

WHY? Orb weavers are spiders that build beautiful spiral webs. These webs are woven in open areas, often between objects, such as tree branches or flower stems. Strands of silk are released from the spider's silk gland, and its spinnerets (silk-spinning organs) are used to form silk lines that radiate out from the center of the web like spokes of a wheel. Coiling silk lines connect the spokes. This web traps flying insects or any insect that might wander into the web. Follow the procedure in the next experiment to study the parts of the web.

Covered

SNARES

PURPOSE To study the strands of an orb web.

MATERIALS orb web from the previous experiment, "Covered"
desk lamp
magnifying lens
pencil with eraser end

PROCEDURE

1. Place the web under the desk lamp.

2. Use the magnifying lens to study the strands of the web. Note the differences in the strands.

3. Gently press the eraser end of the pencil against one of the strands in the web and lift up. Does the web stick to the eraser?

4. Try step 3 again on a different-looking strand.

RESULTS Some of the strands are smooth and some look like a beaded necklace. The beaded strands stick to the pencil eraser.

WHY? The strands of silk in a spiderweb are different. Some spider silk dries when air touches it and some silk stays sticky. The sticky beaded strands are made from a combination of dry and sticky silk. Silk flows out of tiny holes in the spider's spinnerets. The spinnerets move in fingerlike motion as they coat a dry silk strand with sticky silk. The spider then uses the claws on its legs to pluck the strand. The plucking causes the liquid silk to separate into tiny beads along the strand. The sticky strands hold on to any insects that fly or walk into the web until the spider can come and get them. The spider can walk along the dry strands and not get stuck. It also has oil on its feet that prevents it from getting stuck on the sticky strands.

Slow Thinking

PURPOSE To trick your brain.

MATERIALS 5 crayons or markers—red, blue, green, black, and orange
2 sheets of printer paper
timer
helper

PROCEDURE

1. Use each crayon to write the name of another color in a column on the paper as shown. For example, use the green crayon to write Red, the black crayon to write Green, and so on.

2. Ask your helper to time you. When your helper says go, look at the words, but instead of reading the words, identify the color of the letters and say the color out loud. For example, Black is written with a red crayon, so when you look at the printed word Black, say red.

3. Repeat steps 1 and 2, writing the names of animals, such as Bird, Frog, Dog, Fish, and Cat, using a different color for each word.

RESULTS It takes longer to name the color of a written word if the letters spell out a different color than if they spell out other objects such as animals.

WHY? Scientists think that the human brain has one storage place for the names of objects, and another place for the names of colors. When you look at the word Red printed in green, your brain tries to search both of the storage places at once and finds two different answers, which results in a conflict in what to respond. It is much easier and faster to name the colors if the words describe other objects, such as bird, frog, and so on, instead of colors.

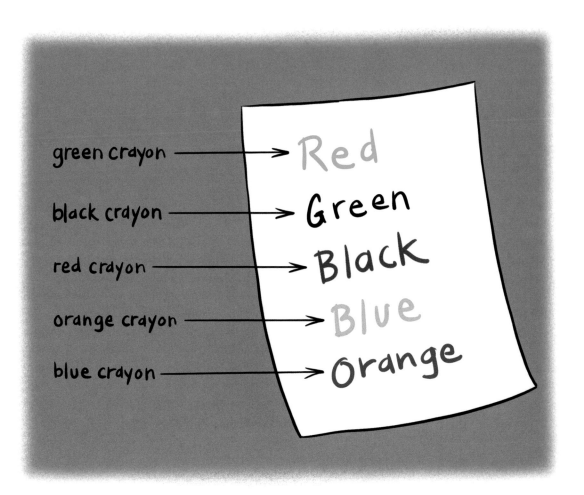

SMELLY

PURPOSE To determine how temperature affects odor.

MATERIALS 4 tablespoons (120 ml) chocolate ice cream

two 5-ounce (150 ml) paper cups

PROCEDURE

1. Place 2 tablespoons (60 ml) of ice cream in each cup.

2. Place one cup in the freezer and leave the other cup sitting at room temperature.

3. Allow the cups to sit undisturbed overnight.

4. Remove the cup from the freezer and smell its contents.

5. Smell the contents of the unchilled cup and compare it to the smell of the other cup's contents.

RESULTS The unchilled ice cream has a stronger chocolate smell.

WHY? Odor is the property of a substance that activates the sense of smell. Materials give off odor when they vaporize, which means they change to a vapor (gas). When a vapor enters your nose, it is picked up by smell detectors, which send a message to your brain. The more vapor that enters the nose at one time, the stronger the smell. The warmer the material, the more it vaporizes and the more its odor gets into your nose. Very cold materials vaporize so little that they have little or no odor.

Smelly

CELL MODEL

PURPOSE To construct a model that shows three parts of a cell.

MATERIALS lemon gelatin dessert mix
1-pint (125 ml) resealable plastic bag
1-quart (1 liter) bowl
large grape
adult helper

PROCEDURE

1. Have your adult helper mix the ingredients for the gelatin dessert according to the instructions on the box.

2. Allow the gelatin to cool to room temperature.

3. Pour the gelatin into the resealable bag, seal the bag, and place it in the bowl.

4. Set the bowl and bag in the refrigerator and chill until the gelatin is firm (about three to four hours).

5. Remove the gelatin from the refrigerator and open the bag.

6. Using your finger, insert the grape into the center of the gelatin.

7. Reseal the bag.

RESULTS A model of a cell with three parts is made.

WHY? All the cells (smallest unit of all living things) in your body, like the model, have these three parts: a cell membrane, cytoplasm, and a nucleus. The plastic bag, like a cell membrane, keeps the parts of the cell together and acts as a barrier to protect the inner parts. The pale color of the gelatin dessert simulates the grayish jellylike material, called cytoplasm, which fills the cell. It is in the cytoplasm that most of the chemical work of the cell takes place. Floating in the gelatin is a grape that represents the nucleus, the cell's governing body. The cell membrane, cytoplasm, and nucleus all work together and are necessary for the life of the cell.

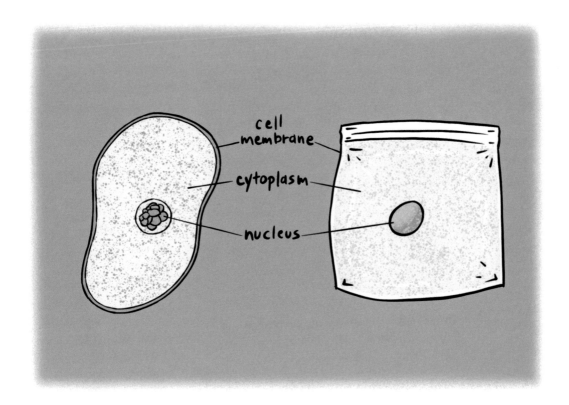

LUB-DUB

PURPOSE To listen to sounds produced by the heart.

MATERIALS cardboard tube from paper towel roll
helper

PROCEDURE

1. In a quiet room, ask your helper to sit in a chair and hold the paper tube against his or her chest. The tube should be slightly to the left side of the chest.

2. Place one of your ears over the other end of the tube.

3. Stand very still and listen to the sound of your helper's heart.

RESULTS Your helper's heart makes a "lub-dub" sound.

WHY? A stethoscope is a medical instrument used to listen to sounds within the body, specifically those made by the heart and lungs. The paper tube works much like the hollow tube stethoscope invented in 1819 by R.T.H. Laennec (1781–1826), a French physician. Heart sounds are the sounds made by the heart's valves (flaps of tissue that control the flow of blood or other liquids in the body) as they shut. The softer "lub" sound is heard when the valves shut in the top chambers of the heart. The louder "dub" sound is heard when the heart valves shut the big vessels leaving the heart.

Lub-Dub

HEARTBEAT

PURPOSE To measure your heart rate.

MATERIALS a watch with a second hand or a timer

PROCEDURE

1. Lay your arm on a table with the palm of your hand up.

2. Place the fingertips of your other hand below the thumb on your upturned wrist.

3. Gently press until you can feel your heartbeat.

NOTE: You may have to move your fingertips around the area until you feel your heartbeat.

4. Count the number of heartbeats that you feel in one minute.

RESULTS A steady beating is felt by the fingertips. The number of beats will vary.

WHY? The number of times your heart beats in one minute is called your heart rate. Adults have an average heart rate of about 70 beats per minute when sitting quietly. Children usually have a faster rate of about 95 beats per minute. The rate for both children and adults increases with activity because your cells need more oxygen and food when you are more active.

SQUEEZED

PURPOSE To demonstrate how hard your heart works.

MATERIALS tennis ball
a watch with a second hand or a timer
paper and pencil
helper

PROCEDURE

1. Hold the tennis ball in one hand.

2. Ask your helper to be the timekeeper. When your helper says start, squeeze the ball as many times as possible, counting each squeeze. When your helper says stop, at the end of 15 seconds, record the number of squeezes. How does your hand feel?

3. Multiply by 4 the number of squeezes in step 2 to determine the number of squeezes that would be made if you kept up the same pace for 60 seconds, or one minute. For example, if you made 40 squeezes in 15 seconds, then: 4 x 40 = 160 squeezes in 60 seconds.

RESULTS The number of squeezes will vary, but squeezing the ball will make your hand feel tired.

WHY? Each time your heart beats, it squeezes about as hard as your hand did in squeezing the tennis ball. At rest, an adult's heart squeezes about 70 times and a child's squeezes about 95 times in one minute. Physical exercise causes the heart to work even harder and squeeze even more times in one minute.

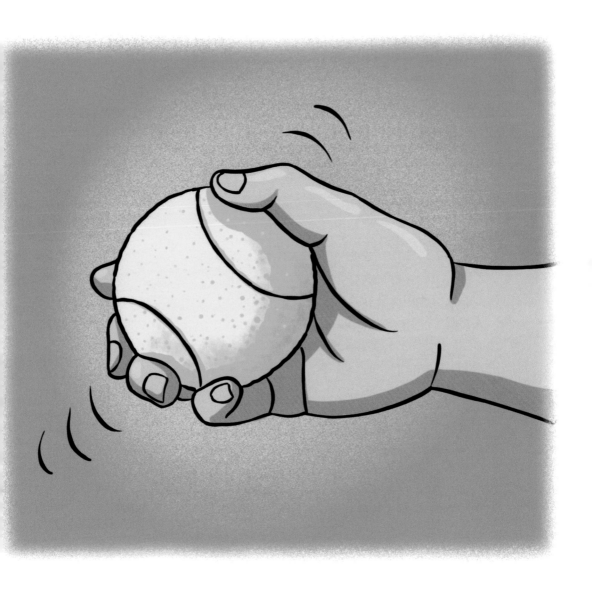

Squeezed

UPHILL

PURPOSE To show the effect of gravity on blood flow.

MATERIALS watch or clock with a second hand or a timer

PROCEDURE

1. Stand against a wall with your left arm held high and your right arm down next to your right side.

2. At the end of one minute, put your hands together palms up.

3. Compare the color of your hands.

RESULTS The right hand is darker than the left hand.

WHY? Gravity pulls everything down, including the blood in your body. The pumping of your heart keeps all the blood from settling at your lowest point, but the heart can't totally compete with gravity. When you hold the left hand up and the right hand down, more blood flows down into the right hand than gets pumped up into the left hand, so the right hand is darker.

GLOSSARY

AMYLASE A complex chemical that breaks down starch into less complex chemicals.

CELL The smallest unit of all living things.

CYTOPLASM The jellylike material that fills a cell.

DIGEST To break down into an absorbable form.

EXTINCT No longer in existence.

HEART RATE The number of times the heart beats in one minute.

LENS A part of the eye that focuses light rays.

MASS The amount of material in an object.

NECTAR A sugary liquid.

NUCLEUS The governing body of a cell.

OMMATIDIUM One of thousands of separate units that make up a compound eye.

OVERFISHING The act of removing fish from a body of water faster than they can reproduce.

OVIPOSITOR An egg-laying tube of an insect or fish.

PRESSURE The amount of force on an area.

PREY An animal hunted for food.

PROBOSCIS A feeding tube in some insects.

SALIVA A liquid in the mouth that softens and breaks down food.

STETHOSCOPE A medical instrument used to listen to sounds inside the body, especially those from the heart and the lungs.

STRIDULATION The process by which insects, such as crickets and grasshoppers, make sounds by rubbing two body parts, usually one sharp-edged and the other rough or file-like, against each other.

VAPORIZE To change to a gas.

FOR MORE INFORMATION

National Geographic Society
  1145 17th Street NW
  Washington, DC 20036-4688
  Museum (202) 857-7700
  Website: http://www.nationalgeographic.com
  The National Geographic Society has been inspiring people to care about the planet since 1888. It is one of the largest nonprofit scientific and educational institutions in the world. Read their magazine for kids, enter the National Geographic Bee, or visit the museum.

National Science Foundation (NSF)
  4201 Wilson Boulevard
  Arlington, VA 22230
  (703) 292-5111
  Website: http://www.nsf.gov
  The NSF is dedicated to science, engineering, and education. Learn how to be a Citizen Scientist, read about the latest scientific discoveries, and discover the newest innovations in technology.

National Zoological Park
  3001 Connecticut Avenue NW
  Washington, DC 20008
  (202) 633-4888
  Website: http://nationalzoo.si.edu
  The National Zoological Park is a part of the Smithsonian Institution, the world's largest museum and research complex. Join a Nature Camp, watch the newest arrivals at the zoo through the Live Animal Cam, or learn more about wildlife research expeditions.

Royal Botanical Gardens
  680 Plains Road West
  Burlington, ON L7T 4H4
  Canada
  (800) 694-4769
  Website: http://www.rbg.ca
  The Royal Botanical Gardens is the largest botanical garden in Canada,
  a National Historic Site, and a registered charitable organization with a
  goal of bringing together people, plants, and nature.

Society for Science and the Public
  Student Science
  1719 N Street NW
  Washington, DC 20036
  (800) 552-4412
  Website: http://student.societyforscience.org
  The Society for Science and the Public presents many science
  resources, such as science news for students, the latest updates on
  the Intel Science Talent Search and the Intel International Science and
  Engineering Fair, and information about cool jobs and doing science.

FOR FURTHER READING

Adamson, Heather. *Emperor Penguins* (Blastoff! Readers: Ocean Life Up Close). Minneapolis, MN: Bellweather Media, Inc., 2018.

Akass, Susan. *My First Science Book: Explore the Wonders of Science with This Fun-Filled Guide*. New York, NY: CICO Kidz, 2015.

Barnes-Svarney, Patricia L. *The Handy Anatomy Answer Book* (The Handy Answer Book Series). Detroit, MI: Visible Ink Press, 2016.

Bunelle, Lynn. *Big Science for Little People*. Boulder, CO: Roost Books, 2016.

Buczynski, Sandy. *Designing a Winning Science Fair Project* (Information Explorer Junior). Ann Arbor, MI: Cherry Lake Publishing, 2014.

Canavan, Thomas. *How Many Cells Are in Your Body?* (Human Body FAQ). New York, NY: PowerKids Press, 2017.

Dickmann, Nancy. *Life Cycles* (Earth Figured Out). New York, NY: Cavendish Square, 2016.

Franchino, Vicky. *Animal Camouflage* (True Book). New York, NY: Children's Press, 2016.

Gray, Leon. *Amazing Animal Engineers* (Fact Finders: Animal Scientists). North Mankato, MN: Capstone Press, 2016.

Hawkins, Jay. *It's Alive! The Science of Plants and Living Things* (Big Bang Science Experiments). New York, NY: Windmill Books, 2013.

Meister, Cari. *Totally Wacky Facts About the Human Body* (Mind Benders). North Mankato, MN: Capstone, 2016.

Moore, Gareth. *Seeing Is Believing* (Brain Benders). Minneapolis, MN: Lerner Publications, 2016.

Stine, Megan. *What Was the Age of Dinosaurs?* (What Was?). New York, NY: Grosset & Dunlap, 2017.

Taplin, Sam. *101 Optical Illusions*. London, England: Usborne Publishing, Ltd., 2016.

Williams, Kathryn. *Plants* (National Geographic Kids Readers). Washington, DC: National Geographic Kids, 2017.

INDEX

Janice VanCleave's Crazy, Kooky, and Quirky Biology Experiments

INDEX